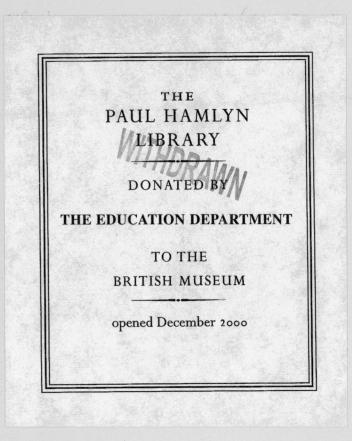

AMAZON INDIANS

Paul Henley

Macdonald Educational

Editor Diana Railton
Consultant John Hemming of the
 Royal Geographical Society, London
Design Roland Blunk
Picture Research Jenny Golden
Production Rosemary Bishop

First published 1980

Macdonald Educational Ltd
Holywell House
Worship Street
London EC2A 2EN

© Macdonald Educational 1980

ISBN 0 356 05954 5

Made and printed by
Waterlow (Dunstable) Limited
England

Artists
Terry Allen Designs Ltd: 4, 12(T), 13
Bryan Evans/Temple Art: 12(B), 24–25,
36–37
Tony Payne: 8, 17, 19, 31
Pat Elliott Shircore: 44–45
George Thompson: 10–11, 34, 35

The publishers are also grateful to the
British Museum for permission to view
part of the Moser/Tayler collection
(page 31).

Cover A member of the Cintas Largas tribe.

Below A river scene in the Amazon Basin.

Contents

The last of the Indians?

Right The tribes living around the Xingu River are famous for their ceremonies. The two men are playing 'long pipes' that make a deep, booming noise. Sometimes, as in this scene, each player has a woman dancing just behind him with one hand on his shoulder.

When Christopher Columbus and his men sailed west from Spain across the Atlantic Ocean in 1492, they were looking for a route to the eastern part of Asia. When they reached land, they thought they had arrived off the coast of India but, in fact, they had become probably the first Europeans to set foot on the soil of the Americas. Columbus mistakenly thought that the native peoples of the Americas were Indians. Today, in order to distinguish them from Asian Indians, they are often called Amer-Indians.

The Amazon Indians

This book is mainly about the Amer-Indians who live in the tropical forest that covers the Amazon Basin of South America. The Amazon Basin is a term for the vast area of land that is drained by the Amazon River and its tributaries. This area is enclosed by the Guiana Highlands in the north and the Brazilian Highlands in the south. Although these highland regions are less forested than the Amazon Basin, all the Indians have a very similar way of life.

The destruction of the forest

Today, large parts of the Amazon forest are being destroyed to make way for roads, towns, cattle ranches and fields. The Indians' way of life depends entirely on the forest. When the trees disappear, their way of life must also disappear. Many people do not care about this. But others point out that the Indians have lived in the forest for thousands of years without destroying it; instead of destroying the Indians' way of life, we should try to learn from it. This book tells you what their way of life is like.

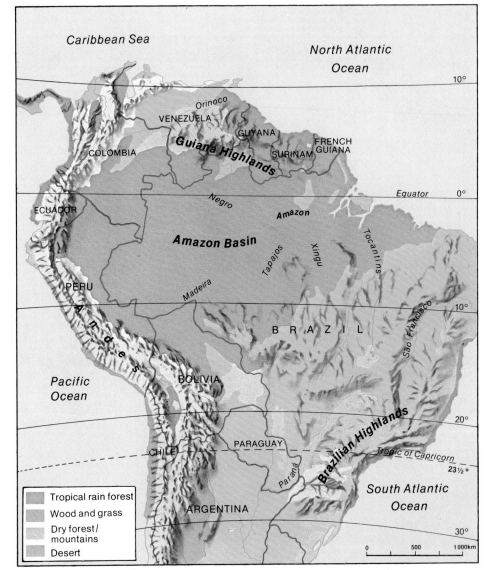

Tropical rain forest
Wood and grass
Dry forest / mountains
Desert

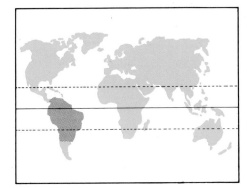

Above The Amazon Basin extends for about 4 million square kilometres in South America. In the heart of this area, continual rainfall has given rise to thick forest vegetation known as 'tropical rain forest'. Away from this area, the rainfall decreases so the vegetation ranges from a thinner layer of forest known as 'tropical dry forest' to sparser forest and grassland, and even desert. You can also see the mountainous areas in the map.

Left The size of the map above in relation to the rest of the world.

The Amazon

Right A river sweeps through thick tropical forest in Brazil – a typical scene in the Amazon Basin.

Below In some rivers in the Amazon Basin, there are so many fish that the Indians need to do very little hunting for meat. These two Kreen Akarore men are gutting the fish they have just caught with a bow and arrow (see page 18). The man on the left is using a steel knife which he would have obtained through trade with non-Indians.

Bottom of page Since one cannot walk for more than a few kilometres in the Amazon Basin without having to cross a river, it is often easier to travel by canoe. Indians particularly use their canoes when they go hunting, fishing, trading or visiting relatives in a distant part of the forest. Here, women are returning home with a heavy gathering of bananas.

Ecology is the study of the way in which all the different parts of the natural environment affect one another and exist together. Besides human beings, and all other living things, the different parts of the natural environment include elements such as the soil, vegetation, rivers and climate. It is necessary to learn a little about the ecological system of the Amazon forest in order to understand how the Indians adapted their way of life to fit in with the natural environment.

A world of rivers

Of all the rivers in the world, the Amazon carries the largest amount of water (the Nile is longer). The Amazon's source lies in the Andes mountains in Peru, close to the Pacific Ocean. From there it flows right across the heart of South America and is joined by over 1,000 tributaries until it reaches the Atlantic Ocean, about 6,500 kilometres away. Its mouth, at the Atlantic, is more than 320 kilometres wide. From it flows one-fifth of all the fresh water entering the world's oceans.

A source of food

The way of life of most Amazon Indians centres around the rivers as the rivers provide them with large quantities of food. In the water itself, there are many species of fish that can be caught for food. Turtles and their eggs are also eaten. The banks of the rivers are good places for hunting as many types of animals live at the water's edge or go there to drink. Also, the best soils for agriculture are often found close to the river banks where layers of fertile silt from the Andes are deposited during floods.

The rain forest

Below In the race for sunlight, the trees of the rain forest can be divided into three main layers.
1 Emergents – a few exceptionally tall trees manage to emerge high above the others.
2 Canopy – the tops of the trees form a dense canopy that prevents most of the sun's light from filtering through.
3 Sub-canopy – the trees compete with one another for the small amount of sunlight that reaches below the canopy.

Bottom of page A section of the rain forest showing the emergent layer of trees above the canopy (see diagram below).

As the Amazon Basin lies astride the Equator, the climate remains hot and humid all the year round. There are only two seasons – the 'wet' and the 'dry'. The dry season lasts for two to three months when only a little rain falls. During the rest of the year, in the wet season, it rains almost every day. Generally the rain comes in short, heavy cloudbursts.

Poor soils

The soils of the Amazon Basin are generally poor. The trees of the rain forest get most of their nourishment from the rain and the sun. This nourishment is mostly held above the ground in the leaves, branches and trunks of the trees. When the trees are cut down, all that is left is a thin layer of poor soil. As the amount of rainfall decreases over South America, the vegetation ranges from thinner forest to open woodland, grassland and scrub.

The trees

The average height of the tallest trees in the rain forest is about 40 metres. They have long, thin trunks, with most of their branches spread out at the top like umbrellas. Since they stand very close to one another, their branches overlap to form a thick canopy. The purpose of the canopy is to catch as much rain and sunlight as possible. As it prevents most of the sun's light from filtering below, inside the forest it is dark and damp; but it is fresh despite the average temperature of about 25 °C. Since all vegetation needs sunlight in order to grow, at ground level there is only a thin layer of young trees and shade-loving plants. There are also many woody, climbing plants, called lianas, that grow up the trunks of trees in order to reach the sunlight.

Below A Cintas Largas family setting off to visit an Indian settlement nearby. Although many small plants and shrubs grow on the forest floor, they are rarely thick or tangled and it is easy to make a path through them. The Indians carry weapons, not only for hunting for food, but also for protection against the dangerous animals of the forest. Inside the forest it is dark and damp. However, it is fresher inside than outside although the temperature averages about 25°C.

The wildlife

All animals (including human beings) depend on plants. Some animals depend on plants directly because they eat them. Other animals depend on plants indirectly because they eat the animals that eat the plants. So the type of wildlife in any part of the world depends to a large extent on the type of vegetation in that area, as well as on the climate.

Distribution of species
In the rain forest, trees and plants of the same species do not usually grow in groups. Instead, many different species are mixed up together. You may have to walk up to a kilometre from one particular type of tree before you find another of the same species. This scattering provides a defence for the trees against the many insects in the forest that attack them.

Most of the animals that the Indians hunt for food eat fruits, buds and fresh leaves. These animals are scattered over the forest in the same way as the trees and plants. They tend to roam the forest by themselves, or in small family groups, rather than in herds. Two important exceptions are the howler monkeys, which live in troops of up to 30, and the peccaries, which are sometimes found in herds of over 100.

Hunting prizes
Generally the animals of the Amazon forest are small. The largest is the tapir which can weigh over 200 kilogrammes. Tapirs, peccaries, monkeys and pacas are all highly prized by the Indians for their meat. Capybaras and brocket deer are hunted near the grassland areas and the river banks. Many types of forest bird also form an important part of the Amazon Indians' diet.

A selection of some of the birds and animals hunted by Amazon Indians for food. *(Not drawn to scale.)* In real life they are not found grouped together like this in one part of the forest. Instead numbers **1-12** are found scattered over large areas of forest, and numbers **13-15** are found in the grassland areas at the edge of the forest.

1 Yellow-headed parrot
2 Toucan
3 Scarlet macaw
4 Great curassow
5 Woolly monkey
6 Howler monkey
7 Spider monkey
8 Night monkey
9 Tamandua
10 Tapir
11 Peccaries
12 Pacas
13 Giant armadillo
14 Brocket deer
15 Capybaras

The first Indians

Human beings are comparative newcomers to the Amazon Basin. Of all the continents, South America was the last to be settled. For literally millions of years, the trees, plants and animals had gradually been developing into their present form. Then, about 30,000 years ago, the first human beings arrived in Alaska during the last great Ice Age. At that time, it was possible to cross over to Alaska from Siberia because the Bering Strait was covered by sheets of ice. These first Amer-Indians and their descendants gradually spread southwards through North and Central America, arriving in South America about 15,000 years ago. As they spread out over the continent, they adopted different ways of life according to the natural environment in which they stayed.

The Andean peoples

When the first Europeans arrived, a mere 500 years ago, there were three main types of Indian society in South America. The central part of the Andean mountain chain was controlled by the Inca Empire. The Incas cultivated their land for crops such as potatoes, maize and beans. They also kept tame animals, such as the llama (a distant relative of the camel), whose wool they used to make clothes. They were ruled by an emperor whom they believed to be a god.

The forest peoples

The peoples living in the forests of the Amazon Basin had a much simpler way of life. They were split up into a large number of tribes that were much smaller than the Inca Empire. Unlike the Inca emperor, their chiefs had very little power.

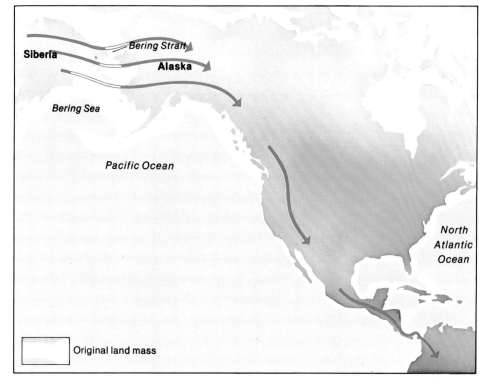

Above Amazon Indians look similar to people from East Asia. This is because they have the same ancestry. The first human beings to arrive in Alaska crossed over from the Asian mainland about 30,000 years ago during the last great Ice Age. The map shows the difference between the shape of the land then and today. Gradually these Indians spread southwards, arriving in South America about 15,000 years ago.

Right When the first Europeans arrived in South America, about 500 years ago, they found the Indians were divided into several different types of society. Each society had developed to meet the conditions of the natural environment in which it was found. The main divisions are shown on the map. Of the many Amazon Indian tribes only the best known, and those mentioned in this book, are shown on the map.

Left The peoples of the Inca Empire of the central Andes cultivated their maize on large terraces which they built on the mountain sides. Also unlike the Amazon Indians, they kept animals, such as the llama, whose wool they used to make clothes.

The Spaniards arrive under Columbus in 1492

Caribbean Sea

North Atlantic Ocean

XINGU TRIBES

JURUNA · KUIKURU
KALAPALO · MEHINAKU
KAMAYURA · SUYA
KAYABI · TXIKÃO
KAYAPO · WAURA
KREEN AKARORE · YAWALAPITI

AMAZON INDIANS
In the forests, they lived by hunting and gathering wild fruits. They grew crops in clearings that they frequently changed.

CARIB
PANARE
YE'KUANA
YANOMAMI · MACUSI
NORTH-WEST AMAZON TRIBES · ATROARI · TIRIO
MAKU
SHUAR · TIKUNA
AGUARUNA · MUNDURUKU · GAVIÕES · CANELA
APINAYE
SHIPIBO · SHERENTE
CAMPA · XINGU TRIBES · KARAJÁ
CINTAS LARGAS · SHAVANTE
NAMBIKUARA
BORORO
INCA EMPIRE

The Portuguese arrive under Cabral in 1500

ANDEAN FARMERS
The peoples living here grew crops in the same areas and kept tame animals. The Incas controlled the central Andes.

GUARANI

Pacific Ocean

South Atlantic Ocean

SOUTHERN NOMADS
In the grasslands and deserts they did not grow crops. They simply wandered over the land, hunting and gathering wild fruits for food.

NORTH-WEST AMAZON TRIBES

BARASANA
CUBEO
DESANA
PIRA-TAPUYA
TANIMUKA
TARIANA
TUKANO
XIRIANA
YUKUNA

0   500   1000km

13

Then the Europeans came

"... These people are very unskilled in arms ... should your Highnesses command it, all the inhabitants could be taken away ... or held as slaves ... for with 50 men we could overpower them all and make them do whatever we wish ..."
Columbus's report to the king and queen of Spain, 12 October 1492.

The above words were written on the day that Columbus landed in the 'New World'. They summarize the attitude that Europeans in America have always had towards the Amer-Indians. Although some Europeans have admired the Indian way of life, this has not prevented most from treating the Indians very cruelly.

Diseases and death
Most of South America was colonized by the Spanish and the Portuguese. They brought with them many diseases which were unknown in the continent before. The Indians had no resistance to these new diseases and, as a result, whole tribes died. Many other tribes died because of the harsh conditions they were forced to work under. Before the arrival of the Europeans, there were probably as many as four million Amazon Indians. Today, there are less than half a million.

The Indians that survived
Almost all the peoples living around the Caribbean and Atlantic coasts died in the first two centuries of European conquest. The small groups living in the southern part of the continent were reduced to a handful. The Spaniards murdered the Inca emperor and made the common people work instead for them. In the Amazon Basin itself, the Portuguese took over the main river banks and destroyed the communities they found there. Only in the parts of the forest away from the main rivers did the Indians remain beyond the reach of the Europeans. It is from these groups, and those that successfully fled from the invaders, that today's surviving Amazon Indians are descended.

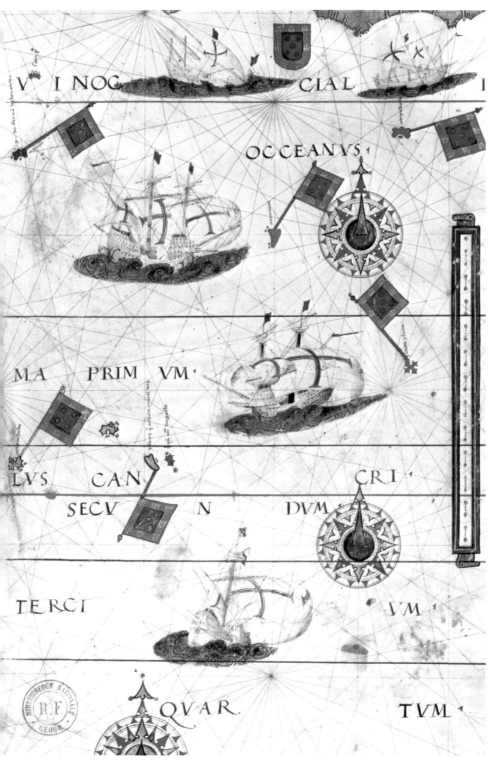

V I NOC ... CIAL I

OCCEANVS

MA PRIM VM

LVS CAN

SECV N DVM

TERCI VM

QVAR TVM

Left This map was drawn by the Portuguese in 1519. Some of the Amazon Indians in the forest are gathering wood for the Portuguese to sell in Europe. You can also see some of the birds and animals of the forest. The Portuguese imagined that there were some very strange creatures there as well! The Portuguese took over all the main river banks in the Amazon Basin. The only Indians who survived were those living away from them deep in the forest.

Below A 16th-century print which shows the Spaniards forcing Indians to act as their bearers.

Above The ruins of a mission in Paraguay. The aim of missionaries was to save the Indians' souls by converting them to Christianity. They used to gather Indian groups into colonies around their missions. This brought the Indians into even closer contact with European diseases. Some missions had to be abandoned because the Indians in the area had all died. This one, belonging to Jesuits, was abandoned in the 18th century when the king of Spain ordered the Jesuits to leave South America because he was afraid that they were beginning to exercise too much control over the Indians.

Gardens in the forest

Below A garden that is just about to be planted. The tree trunks which have not been completely burnt are left lying on the ground and the crops are planted between them.

Bottom of page Clearing the garden for their families is the men's work but most of the planting and harvesting is done by the women. Here Txikão women are digging up manioc.

Most Indian tribes today depend on 'slash and burn' agriculture to grow much of their food. During the dry season the men of each family slash down part of a small area of forest for their family (about one hectare each). The fallen tree trunks and leaves are left to dry in the sun. Shortly before the wet season begins, this debris is set alight. The ashes from the fire act as fertilizer for the poor soil. As soon as the ashes have cooled down, planting can begin.

Mixing crops

The Indian families plant a large variety of food crops in their sections of the garden. The most important are manioc, maize and bananas. Less important, but also very frequent, are yams, papayas, sweet potatoes, peanuts, pineapples and sugar cane. The Indians also plant crops which are not edible but which have other uses. These include tobacco, cotton, and plants used in medicines and poisons.

Moving the gardens

After a garden has been in use for about three years, the crops are prevented from growing properly by a large number of weeds that have appeared. It is then less work for the Indians to abandon that garden and start a new one elsewhere. The forest gradually reclaims the abandoned garden, but the banana trees continue to produce fruit for many years. Once the forest has returned to its full height, the Indians are able to cut it down again and use the same plot of land as a garden. Abandoning a garden every two or three years enables the forest to reclaim that land before the soil has become exhausted and, as a result, infertile.

Above An Indian village usually has several gardens, each at a different stage of growth, within easy walking distance of its settlement. The peoples of the settlement above (**1**) have just cut a new garden (**2**). Garden (**3**) is already one year old and almost all the crops are ready for harvesting. Only the banana trees are too small to produce fruit. Garden (**4**) is over two years old. All the crops have been harvested except for the banana trees which now dominate the garden. Garden (**5**) is a very old one which the Indians abandoned after about three years. This was so that the forest could reclaim it before its soil became exhausted. In time the same site will be used again as a garden. *(Not drawn to scale.)*

Right Some of the crops that the Amazon Indians grow in their gardens:

Manioc roots are either boiled or turned into flour from which bread is made.

Maize grains are removed from the cob and boiled up into a rich soup.

Cotton is spun into thread by the women who use it to weave hammocks and loincloths.

Tobacco leaves are rolled into cigars or turned into wads that are sucked.

Peanuts are usually eaten as a snack and rarely form part of a main meal.

Pineapples are usually eaten raw and as a snack rather than as a main meal.

Manioc

Maize

Cotton

Tobacco

Peanuts

Pineapple

Hunting and fishing

Below The Panare, like many other tribes, use poisonous plants for catching fish. The plants are crushed and put in a basket in a small river so that their poison is released in the water. As it is carried downstream, it dazes the fish making them move very slowly. It is then quite easy to spear them with the harpoons seen sticking out of the water in the background. Eating the poisoned fish does not harm the Indians.

Most Amazon Indians use a wooden club, a bow and arrow, or a lance, for hunting animals. The arrows and lances traditionally have bone or wooden heads. Today some tribes use metal heads made from tools traded with non-Indians. Shotguns are also being acquired by trade.

Skills

Successful hunting requires great skill at tracking and knowledge of the ways of life of the animals in the forest. Since the animals are usually scattered over the forest in ones or twos, Indians generally go hunting alone or in small groups. However, as peccaries often live in large herds, when a hunter spots their tracks in the forest he will go back to his village and call the other men. They will then help him to surround and kill the animals.

Some Indians become skilled at using a bow and arrow for shooting fish. When doing this, they have to remember that all objects in the water appear to be nearer the surface than they actually are. So the Indians have to aim into the water a little below where the fish appears to be in order to hit it.

Hunting with poisoned darts

Blowpipes are used for killing birds and monkeys, high up in the canopy of the trees, with poisoned darts. A dart is inserted in the hollow, wooden pipe. Then only a slight puff of breath is needed to blow the dart up to about 30 metres. The point of the dart is very sharp and is covered with curare, a poison made from a wild forest plant. When the dart enters the animal's body, the curare slowly paralyses its muscles and, eventually, its lungs so that it dies because it cannot breathe.

Below A Tukano man using a blowpipe to kill a bird in the canopy with a poisoned dart. Only a slight puff through the mouthpiece will send the dart up to a target as far away as 30 metres. Using a blowpipe is not easy. Successful hunters require a lot of practice and skill. The man in the foreground carries a bow and arrows. It is only the men who go hunting with weapons, but women and children join in and enjoy fish-poisoning expeditions.

Right Some of the Amazon Indians' weapons. *(Not drawn to exact scale.)*
1 Lance with metal head.
2 Lance with wooden head.
3 Bow, with cord made from tree bark, and arrows.
4 Blowpipe and mouthpiece.
5 Quiver for blowpipe darts.
6 Darts wrapped with cotton-like material so that they fit neatly into the blowpipes.

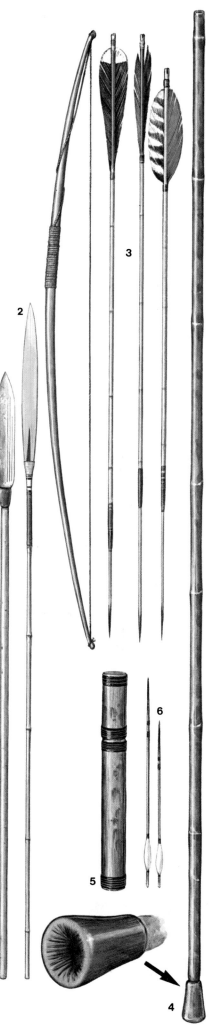

Harvesting the forest

Although the Indians get most of their food from their gardens or from hunting and fishing, they add to their supply with food gathered directly from the forest.

A variety of snacks

Many trees in the forest produce small edible fruits which the Indians eat as snacks or turn into drinks by crushing them in water. Particularly important are the fruits that grow on palm trees. The Indians often have to climb to the tops of trees to cut the fruits down. A sweet drink is made by diluting wild honey with water. There are many different types of honey-making bee in the Amazon forest but, fortunately for the Indians, most of these bees do not sting.

Other snacks that the forest provides include fat white grubs, found in the trunks of rotting palm trees, and large flying ants. Both of these are usually roasted before being eaten. This gives them a nutty flavour.

Useful materials

It is not only food that the Indians gather from the forest. From the trunks and branches of the trees they make the frames of their houses, canoes, cooking utensils and stools. Palm leaves are used for thatching the roofs of their houses. The canes found growing beside forest streams are used to make baskets and the shafts of arrows and lances. The sap of certain trees is used as gum for sticking feathers to the shafts of arrows. Tree barks are turned into loincloths, straps for carrying baskets and cords. Many different types of plant are used to make medicines and poisons.

20

Below A Maku man making curare, the poison used on blowpipe darts, from the bark of a forest shrub. He is using an aluminium bowl obtained through trade.

Right One Kayapo girl painting another with the black paint known as genipa. The red paint they have on their faces is called urucu. Genipa is made from a wild fruit and urucu from the seeds of a forest bush. Among the Kayapo, and most other tribes, men and women paint their bodies in different ways. They wear body paint at all times of year but take more care in applying it when they are preparing for ceremonies.

Below A Tukano man lighting a torch made from beeswax.

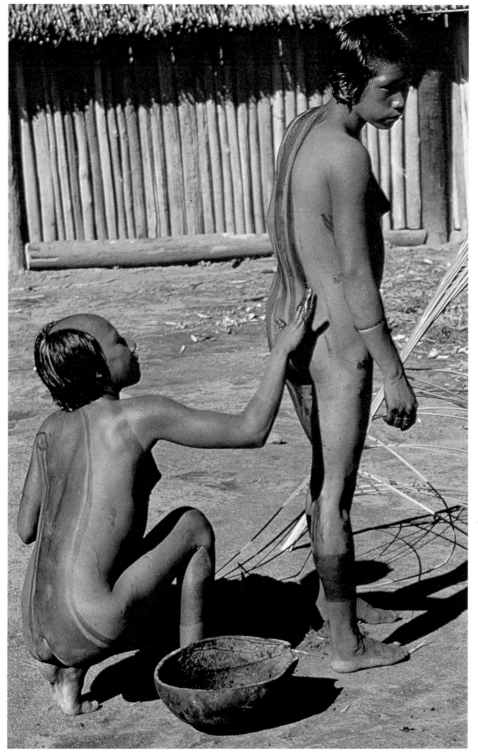

Villages

Below A Kayapo village in central Brazil. Each of the houses arranged in a square is the home of several families. Behind the family houses, there are a number of small huts in which the women of the village do the cooking. The hut in the centre of the square is a meeting place for the men of the village.

When the Indians want to build a village, they begin by cutting a clearing in the forest close to a river or stream. They then build a wooden frame in the clearing (see page 35), lashed together with lianas, and completely cover it with palm thatch. They usually make a smoke hole at the top of the house, and one or two narrow slits in the side for doors. But there are no windows, so the house is dark and cool inside. Several families live in each house.

The size of Indian villages

In some villages in central Brazil, there are six or more large family houses arranged in a square or circle. Beside these large houses, there may be several small huts in which the women do their cooking. In the centre, there is often another small hut used by the men as a sort of club-house. These villages sometimes have as many as 300 inhabitants. But most Amazon Indian villages are much smaller, having no more than 50 inhabitants and only one or two large family houses.

Moving villages

After about five years, the palm thatch of a house begins to rot, and lets in the rain. If the Indians have recently started a garden nearby, they will build a new house close to the old one. However, if their gardens are growing old, or if the animals they hunt have become scarce, they will build a new house a few kilometres away. Then the forest will take over their old gardens and the animal population will begin to increase again. So, by moving the site of their houses every few years, the Indians never totally exhaust the resources that the natural environment provides.

Left A Panare village, consisting of only one large house in which all the 30 members of the group live.

Right Part of the thatch, made from dried palm leaves, on the inside of a Tanimuka house. After about five years, the thatch begins to rot and let in the rain. It is often easier for the Indians to build a new house, since this only takes a few weeks, rather than to go on repairing the old one.

Families in the forest

Inside an Indian house, each family has its own open fireplace close to one of the side walls. At night, each member of the family goes to sleep around the fire. Everybody has a hammock to sleep in except for very small children who sleep with their mothers. When a boy reaches the age of about 12, he leaves his family's fireplace and hangs his hammock in the central part of the house which is the space reserved for young bachelors. A girl sleeps by her family's fireplace until she marries.

Marriage

Girls marry when they are between 15 and 18 years old, while boys marry when they are between 18 and 22. If a boy wants to marry a particular girl, he must ask her parents first. The parents discuss the matter with their daughter and, if she agrees, the boy moves into their house. There is no special marriage ceremony. The girl simply builds her own fireplace, close to her mother's, and she and her husband hang their hammocks around it. An Indian man often has more than one wife.

The women

Indian men do most of their work outside the village. The women plant and harvest the gardens, take part in fish-poisoning expeditions, and gather fruits from the forest. However, most of their work is done in the villages – cooking, looking after the children, gathering firewood, and keeping the house tidy. They also spend much time weaving hammocks and loincloths. After the men have built the houses, they then do little work in the village besides weaving baskets, carving wooden tools and mending their weapons.

Indians share most of the food they produce. Each wife cooks the meat which her husband has caught that day, and the vegetables which she has gathered from the gardens. She then divides the food into two parts – one for her husband to share with the men and the remainder for her to share with the women, girls and younger boys. The picture shows Panare men having their meal inside the main village house. On the left is some bread made from manioc. A pet macaw looks on. The Indians' few possessions are stored in baskets on the beams.

Growing up

" Make children and they will help you later. They will get fish for you when they grow up and you are old."
Akusa, Mehinaku chief, in a public speech.

An Indian man never relies on another man to do a job for him, nor does a woman ever rely on another woman. A grown-up has to know how to do everything that is expected of someone of his or her own sex.
If a baby is born with a deformity it is killed because, later on, it would not be able to look after itself. Only when they are very old do the Indians rely on other people.

Learning adult skills
Every Indian child has a lot to learn. A boy has to learn in particular how to make and use hunting weapons, how to spot animal tracks, how to choose the best site for a garden or a village clearing, where to find useful materials in the forest, how to build houses and how to weave baskets.
A girl has to learn in particular how to plant crops and tend them as they grow, where to find wild fruits, what wood makes good firewood, how to prepare food, how to spin cotton and weave hammocks, and how to look after young children.
But Indian children do not learn all these things by going to school. Instead they learn by copying their parents or by playing together.

Learning through play
Many of the games played by Indian children help them to prepare for adult life. Boys are given miniature bows and arrows and they practise how to shoot well by aiming at lizards. Girls are given miniature baskets in which they bring back food from the gardens. Boys and girls usually play separately.
However, Indian children also play games just for fun. In fact it was the Indians who, long ago, invented ball games by using balls made of wild rubber from the forest trees.

Below A Cintas Largas child watches her mother grate manioc roots. The pulp will eventually be turned into the flour from which manioc bread is made. Indian children are allowed to join in almost all grown-up activities, including hunting and fishing, but they are never forced to do so. Indian parents never spank their children even if they are rude!

Above A group of Nambikuara boys on a hunting expedition of their own. Although these expeditions are never very serious, they help the boys to acquire skill and experience in tracking and killing animals. When they are adults, they will depend on their hunting ability for their meat.

Left A Kreen Akarore girl gathering wood from her family's garden. Boys lead a very carefree life, but girls are kept busy helping their mothers with their daily chores.

Initiation

"Look, we are happy now because this is how the first people of long ago did things."
Manyen, a Panare man, during a boys' initiation ceremony.

Below A Karajá girl during the final stage of her initiation ceremony when she is dressed up in loincloth and beads, and other decorations, and her body is painted. The initiation ceremonies held by Indian tribes all differ. Carib girls, for example, remain inside the house throughout all the stages of the ceremony and the celebrations are held around them.

In many tribes, children have an 'initiation' ceremony which symbolizes the fact that they are about to enter adulthood. The age at which they are initiated varies from tribe to tribe. Some tribes have initiation ceremonies for girls, others have them for boys, but some have them for both.

The Carib girl's ceremony
When a Carib girl is about 14 years old, her mother builds her a small hut of palm leaves within the family house. The girl must remain inside this hut for eight days, without talking to anyone and just spinning cotton.

At the end of eight days, the girl's mother invites to the house an elderly couple who are known to be hard workers. The girl comes out of her hut and the old woman places some cotton in her hands and sets light to it. In order not to get scorched, the girl quickly throws the cotton from hand to hand until it is all burnt up. Then the old man takes the girl's hands and puts them for a moment in a small bowl filled with large, biting ants.

The purpose of these stages in the ceremony is to remind the girl that she should be a hard worker. When handling cotton, her hands should always move quickly just as they did when she tossed the burning cotton from hand to hand during the ceremony. In all other aspects of life she should also work hard, just as the ants in the bowl are thought to.

Finally, the girl is dressed up in a loincloth, necklaces, bracelets and earrings, and her body is painted. Other visitors are served manioc beer and dance and sing while the girl watches from her hammock.

Left A Panare man decorating a loincloth specially woven so that it can be worn by a boy during his initiation ceremony.

Below While everyone else is singing and dancing, the boys who are to be initiated have to stand perfectly still, leaning on sticks, at the edge of the dancing area. Behind them stand the young men who guide them through all the stages of the ceremony. You can also see the loincloths, beads and headdresses that the boys will put on later in the ceremony.

Bottom left A boy being dressed in a loincloth for the first time. While this is happening, he must cover his eyes because it is believed that he may die if he sees a woman.

Bottom right A Panare boy completely dressed at the end of the ceremony. From now he will wear a loincloth for the rest of his life. Although the loincloth is regarded as a symbol of adulthood, the boy still has a lot to learn before he will be considered grown-up.

The Panare boy's ceremony

Panare boys go through an initiation ceremony when they are between 8 and 12 years old. The most important part of this ceremony is the dressing of each boy for the first time in a loincloth, with bead armbands and other decorations that symbolize that he is about to become an adult. The ceremony is carried out in stages during three large, public dances, held during the dry season. Each dance lasts for 24 hours, from nightfall until nightfall, but there are breaks of several weeks between them.

During the dances, the initiation ceremony is mixed with the celebration of hunting, fishing and crop growing. Most of the songs sung during the first two dances are about the animals and fish that the Panare eat. For much of the time, the boys have to stand completely still at the edge of the dancing area.

In the third dance, however, the initiation of the boys becomes the centre of attention. The day before the dance, the boys are taken into the forest where they are given special medicines to make them strong. The songs in the third dance are about the things that the boys will wear for the first time. The following afternoon, the boys are dressed by men who have been specially invited from other villages. Afterwards everyone, except the boys, joins together in a huge feast of smoked meat and manioc bread.

The next day, the newly initiated boys go out into the forest alone for the first time. But although they now dress like adults, they will not be considered grown-up until they have learnt how to hunt, fish and make clearings in the forest.

Music and dancing

*"Put more beer
In this beautiful bowl.
Let us dance, my little wife."
A Shuar dance song.*

Opposite Some of the Amazon Indians' musical instruments.

Below Tribes in the north-west of the Amazon Basin, like the Tukano in the photograph, dance in mixed lines with their arms round one another's backs. Several men shake maracas in time to the chanting. In the large villages in central Brazil, men and women usually dance in separate lines in the large open space in front of their houses. Often the dancers are led by two men playing long pipes (see page 5).

In addition to initiation ceremonies, Amazon Indians have ceremonies on many other occasions—for example, after a death, or when a new garden has been cleared or a house has been built. In all these ceremonies, both music and dancing play an important part.

Musical instruments

Amazon Indians play wind and percussion instruments. They do not use stringed instruments. Almost all tribes play a flute of some sort, made either from bamboo or from the hollow leg bone of an animal. Some tribes play their flutes through the nose rather than through the mouth. A nose flute produces a very delicate, high note. Most tribes also play panpipes. By blowing along the row of pipes, the player produces a scale of different notes. Completely different are the long pipes which are played by the tribes that live in the Xingu River region and in the Guiana Highlands. They make a deep, booming noise like a horn.

The most common percussion instrument is the maraca. When it is shaken, the seeds or pebbles inside it produce a rattling sound. Like most musical instruments, the maraca is usually played only by the men.

Dancing

When Indians dance, they do not skip about or jump up and down. Instead, they move in quick, short steps, almost like walking. They generally dance in lines rather than in couples, like the people in the photograph on the right. The Indians usually only sing when they are dancing. Their songs are mostly complicated chants with notes that change only slightly.

Bamboo long pipes. They produce a deep, booming noise like a horn and are played in pairs.

A drum made from animal skin stretched over part of a hollow tree trunk.

From top to bottom: Bamboo mouth flutes; a deer bone whistle; and bamboo panpipes.

Maracas made from a small gourd and filled with seeds or pebbles.

A rattle worn around the ankle, made from nutshells.

Spirits of the forest

Below A Yanomami shaman treating a sick person. He is trying to draw out the invisible object believed to have been blown into the victim's body by an evil spirit.

Amazon Indians do not believe in a single god who governs and controls everything. Instead they believe in the existence of a large number of spirits of different kinds. Some of these are mentioned on page 35.

The power of the spirits

Most tribes believe that an invisible spirit lives in each person's body. When a person dies the spirit is believed to leave his or her body. Many tribes believe that animals and plants also have spirits.

Spirits are believed to be able to leave the bodies in which they normally live, even before someone dies, and to wander about the forest in an invisible form. The Indians consider them dangerous because they can cause sickness or death by blowing invisible darts, or other objects, into people's bodies. The Indians are therefore afraid to come into contact with these spirits and do not pray to them.

Shamans

The Indians do not separate religious activities and everyday life as much as we do. Unlike us, they have no special temples and no special class of priests. However, some Indians are considered by their tribes to be particularly knowledgeable about the activities of spirits. They are called shamans and are nearly always men. Many shamans take drugs to help them see the spirits that are invisible to other people. A shaman is thought to be able to cure people by sucking or drawing out the invisible objects that spirits have blown into their bodies. But a shaman does not dress in any special way and has no special privileges. He also does the same work as every other man.

Right A shrunken head – a trophy of the Shuar. The mouth has been sewn up to prevent the spirit of the victim escaping and taking revenge upon the person who killed him.

Shrinking heads

The Shuar were once famous for their practice of shrinking their enemies' heads. They believed that the spirit inside each man gave him a store of mysterious power. However, a man's store of power was believed to be decreasing all the time and, when it had all gone, he would die. The only way a man could build up his store of power, and not die, was by killing his enemies. But the danger of this was that the spirits of the dead enemies might then escape and take revenge upon the killers by causing them sickness or death. The Shuar therefore used to cut off their enemies' heads, shrink them, and sew up their mouths so that the spirits could not escape from them and cause harm.

First the skin and flesh were removed from the victim's skull and sewn together in one piece. Then, heated pebbles and sand were poured into the skull-less head so that it would dry out and shrink. This was done time and time again until it had shrunk to about the size of a man's fist. The killer would then wear his trophy round his neck during the celebrations that followed a raid.

It seems that the Shuar gave up shrinking heads after they came into greater contact with non-Indians in the 1960s.

Right The masks worn by these Yawalapiti dancers represent spirits connected with special ceremonies. It is essential that the wearers of the masks are completely disguised in order to keep the strong link between the Indians and the spirits. That is why the dancers have covered themselves up in woven straw.

In the beginning...

"They have many stories, the old people, they are our memory."
A Maku man.

The Indians have many different legends and beliefs. These explain various puzzles like how the world and the first people came into being, how fire was discovered, and how the universe is constructed. These stories are told at night by the old people. They have been passed down from parents to children for countless generations.

The Kayapo learn about fire

This legend is told by the Kayapo and many other tribes of central Brazil.

'Long ago, human beings did not know how to make fire. Instead of cooking meat, they cut it into thin strips and laid it out to dry in the sun.

One day, a boy named Botokue went out to hunt for macaws with his brother-in-law. They spotted a nest high up on a steep rock. They made a ladder out of a tree trunk and Botokue climbed up to the nest. When he reached the nest, he found that the birds had flown away. Botokue shouted down to his brother-in-law that there was nothing left in the nest but stones. But his brother-in-law did not believe him and called him a liar. They began to quarrel. Botokue got annoyed and started throwing stones down at his brother-in-law. This made the brother-in-law so angry that he pulled away the ladder and went off home in a huff.

Botokue was left stranded on the rock. There was no way he could get down. Weeks went by and he was on the point of starvation when a jaguar passed by at the foot of the rock. Botokue was frightened of the jaguar and kept very quiet. But the jaguar saw Botokue's shadow and looked up. To Botokue's surprise, the jaguar was able to talk. He was also very friendly. The jaguar scrambled up the rock to the nest and told Botokue to sit on his back. Then he took Botokue off to his home in the forest.

At the jaguar's home there was a large fire with meat being cooked over it. The jaguar gave some to Botokue. It was the first cooked meat he had ever eaten and it tasted delicious! The jaguar said that he could stay as long as he liked. But the jaguar's wife did not like Botokue being there. One day, when her husband was out hunting, she attacked the boy. In self-defence, he pulled out his bow and arrow and shot her dead. He was then afraid that the jaguar would kill him when he returned. So he ran off home to his own village.

His family was pleased to see him again but did not believe his story. They insisted on going back to the jaguar's home to steal the fire. This they did and, since that day, the Kayapo have always cooked their meat. But the jaguar was very angry with them for stealing the fire. That is why jaguars today are so full of hatred for human beings and often attack them in the forest.'

The Tanimuka universe

The Tanimuka think of the universe as a vast house resting on the earth, just as their own houses do. The earth is believed to be supported by a huge boa constrictor. All around the boa constrictor is an endless expanse of water.

Above the earth, there are five worlds believed to be the same as the Tanimuka's world, except that they are inhabited by spirits. The spirits of each world live in houses which have the same structure as the Tanimuka's. Most spirits are believed to be capable of moving between their world and the Tanimuka's.

The sun is believed to cross the sky at the level of the world of the spirits of music. Because the three spirit worlds below are invisible, the Tanimuka's world still receives light from the sun's rays. But the rays do not reach the world of the creator spirits who inhabit the very top of the universe. For this reason, they live in permanent darkness.

When the sun sets in the west, it is thought to be about to pass underneath the earth and the boa constrictor that supports it. It does this by travelling in a canoe across the water. In the morning it rises again in the east.

A jaguar.

Left The wooden frame of a Tanimuka house. The Tanimuka believe that the universe has the same structure as their houses.

Right A Tanimuka house, ready to live in after being thatched.

Below The structure of the universe, according to the Tanimuka. A vast house, consisting of six worlds, rests on the earth which is supported by a huge boa constrictor. The sun's rays never reach the top world. At night, the sun crosses the water by canoe.

1 *World of the spirits that created the world of the Tanimuka*

2 *World of the spirits of music*

3 *World of the spirits of the dead and vultures*

4 *World of the spirits of forest plants and wild animals*

5 *World of the spirits of cultivated plants*

6 *World of the Tanimuka*

Chiefs and warriors

"I am a jaguar,
The bravest that is,
And no one
Can get near my house."
A Shuar shaman's song.

The chiefs of Amazon Indian tribes generally have very little power. They lead by example, rather than by command. For instance, if the area around a house needs to be cleared of weeds, a chief will start the work himself and then call others to join him. A chief is expected to be a reasonable person who can settle the disputes among the other members of his settlement.

A chief is respected but he enjoys no special privileges. In most tribes, the chief does not dress in any special way. Also, like the shaman, a chief does the same work as every other man. In fact the chiefs are often, but not always, shamans as well.

Raids

Most tribes are very peaceable and regard violence as the worst sort of behaviour. But a few tribes, like the Shuar and Yanomami, have earned a reputation for being warriors. Whole tribes do not now go to war against one another. Instead, warfare usually consists of raids by the members of one village on another village of the same tribe.

The Yanomami

One of the few tribes that still practises warfare is the Yanomami. Often, the only reason for a raid is because one village wishes to take revenge upon another village for an earlier raid. But sometimes the aim of a raid is to capture wives. From time to time, when there are not enough women to provide wives for all the men, these men will raid a neighbouring village, killing the men who live there and capturing the young women. The young women are taken home by the raiders and made to become their wives.

36

A group of Yanomami warriors, armed with bows and arrows, about to leave to raid a neighbouring village. A raiding party of this kind may have to walk for one or two days before getting close to the enemies' village. They will then hide in the forest overnight. As soon as it is light enough to see, they will set upon the enemies' village, hoping that the men will still be asleep in their hammocks and therefore unable to defend themselves.

Crafts and trade

"They have things that are really beautiful, and we have things that they like. And so we trade, and that is good."
Kuyaparei, a Mehinaku man, explaining why his tribe trades with the Waura.

Below On special occasions, Tukano men wear headdresses made of toucan, macaw and crane feathers. Many different types of headdress are made. Compare the one below with those on pages 5 and 29.

Amazon Indians do not make objects so that they can just look at them. Instead, their objects have daily practical purposes. Often the objects which they wear or use in ceremonies are made from perishable materials, like feathers, and have to be re-made each time a ceremony is held. But they are very beautiful and made with care.

No specialists
In all tribes, men and women make different things. For example, in some tribes the men may weave baskets while the women make pottery. In other tribes, however, it may be the men who make pottery and the women who weave baskets. But there are no specialized craftspeople. Each man and each woman knows how to make the different things that are traditionally made by someone of his or her sex.

Trade
Some tribes are known for being good at making a particular object. For example, the tribes who live in the Guiana Highlands are famous for being good basket-makers; the tribes who live in the north-west of the Amazon Basin, like the Barasana, are famous for their pottery. When two tribes that are good at making different things live close to one another, they will trade by exchanging their craftwork.

Nowadays, many tribes trade their craftwork for goods brought by non-Indian traders. The objects the Indians particularly want include steel tools, aluminium cooking pots, and coloured glass for beads. The non-Indian traders do not use the objects that the Indians have made. Instead, they sell them to townspeople and foreign tourists.

Right Masks worn by Tanimuka dancers when they represent the spirits of the forest (see page 33).Each dancer puts the mask completely over his head. He is able to breathe through the holes made around the nose. He will also cover himself up with a woven straw costume, like the dancers on page 33.

Left A Tirio girl weaving a cotton hammock. Before beginning to weave, a girl has to pick a very large ball of cotton and then clean it and spin it into thread. In all, the weaving of a hammock requires several weeks' work.

Right A Maku woman weaving a carrying basket out of cane. Although the Maku use these baskets themselves, they also trade them with neighbouring Tukano Indians, and with missionaries and traders.

Below A Barasana man painting one of the clay pots for which his tribe is famous. Pottery is usually baked over an open fire, painted, and then varnished with the sap from a tree. The bead necklace the man is wearing is made of coloured glass that was obtained from non-Indians.

The invasion continues

"We have the right to live in our land here . . . We are the true Brazilians, not the whites. The whites came to fill up this land, to put an end to us, this is what they want . . ." Tsererobo, Shavante chief, 1978.

Below A Tirio village that has grown up around a Protestant mission. Encouraged by the missionaries, the Indians usually live in small one-family houses, instead of the large communal houses.

Bottom of page Many tribes have been moved into special areas to make way for the roads that are being built through their homelands. It is not easy for the Indians to adjust to these new conditions. Many have died from diseases caught from non-Indians.

The Amazon Indian tribes that have managed to keep their traditional way of life live in areas that are isolated from the rivers most accessible to the outside world. Until recently, non-Indian settlers found it very difficult to get into these isolated areas. Even if they succeeded, they found it even more difficult to establish permanent settlements there.

The new invaders

Today, however, the non-Indian settlers are armed with all sorts of modern equipment that the earlier settlers did not have. For example, two-way radios provide contact with other parts of the country, and light aircraft bring supplies to remote areas. Since the late 1960s, powerful modern bulldozers and earthmovers have been cutting wide, new roads through the forest.

The effect on the Indians

These new invaders have affected the Indians almost as badly as did the first Europeans who settled along the river banks in the 16th and 17th centuries. Much of the Indians' lands has been taken from them and the forest chopped down to make way for roads, towns, fields and cattle ranches. Missionaries have persuaded many Indians that their traditional way of life was sinful, that they should change their spiritual beliefs and wear clothes.

Faced with the modern world, many Indians have lost confidence in their own traditions. Once the forest has been chopped down, they have no way of making their own living. Instead, many Indians have turned to begging along the new roads, or in the nearby towns, in order to stay alive.

Below A bulldozer working on one of the roads running through the centre of the Amazon Basin. This particular road runs directly through the lands of the Atroari who have killed more than 20 people, mostly road workers or government officials, sent to pacify them.

Right The new roads through the forest have provided access to many areas where there are valuable minerals, including gold, iron, copper, lead and diamonds. The photograph shows a diamond miner panning with a sieve in a stream. Mines usually do not take over as much of the forest as fields and cattle ranches.

Working for the future

'We are tired of waiting. Our reserves are devastated, without wood. Who took it? Was it the Indians, to make their houses? No, it was the white man. We can no longer keep our arms folded. Perhaps this is the last time we will be able to rise up as tribes, to raise the voices of our tribes . . .'

These words come from a speech by Tupa-y, a Guarani Indian, made after his tribe's reserve in southern Brazil had been ransacked by logging companies in 1977.

Indian land rights

More important than anything else to the Amazon Indians is their land. Without land, no tribe can survive. In most of the countries where the Amazon Indians live, their rights to their lands are recognized by law. But more often than not, the law is not enforced.

In Brazil, certain areas of land have been marked out as Indian reserves. Each reserve has a government agent who is supposed to make sure that the Indians' land is not invaded by outsiders and to help the Indians to adjust to being part of modern Brazil. Some of these agents have worked hard to help the Indians defend their rights, but others have allowed the invasion of Indian lands to continue.

The most famous Brazilian reserve covers 20,000 square kilometres of land around the Xingu River, and is known as the Xingu Indian Park. It was set up in 1959 by Claudio and Orlando Villas Boas, who dedicated most of their lives to helping the Indians. The tribes living in this reserve are able to lead their normal lifestyle within its boundaries.

Below A Tirio nurse, trained by Protestant missionaries, at work in her clinic. Protestant missionaries, who are mostly North Americans, have provided several Indian tribes with medical attention. In other parts of South America, the Indians in reserves are given medical treatment. The diseases that have affected the Indians very bady include smallpox, measles and tuberculosis.

Conflict with the modern world

Despite the harsh treatment that they have received, most Indians wish to remain in contact with the modern world. The modern world has certain goods to offer that the Indians now appreciate very much—besides steel tools and aluminium cooking pots, these include outboard motors, radios and modern medicine.

Many Indians want to learn about the outside world so that they can understand what is happening in the Amazon Basin today. But they complain bitterly that nearly all contact with non-Indians leads to their land being stolen. At the same time, most Indians are proud to belong to their different tribes and do not want to lose their identity.

Recently, the invasion of Indian lands in Brazil has become so bad that the Indians have begun to hit back. Some Indians have attacked the settlers invading their reserves. Several Indian tribes have joined together to form a federation of chiefs to voice their complaints.

The future?

Large and powerful companies are also invading the Indians' lands. These companies produce valuable minerals, timber, meat and coffee, and other useful things, that can be exported to North America, Europe and Japan. In other words, it is partly for the sake of people in these countries that the forest is being chopped down and the traditional way of life of the Indians is being destroyed. Unless a way is found to combine the protection of the Indians' interests with further plans for economic development in the future, it seems unlikely that they will be able to survive for another two or three generations.

Left In order to acquire the goods that they want from the outside world, the Indians must have something to trade. Alternatively, they must work for a wage like this Shavante who is working in a sawmill at the São Marcos mission.

Below Claudio Villas Boas (centre) who, with his brother Orlando, for many years supervised the Indian reserve in Brazil known as the Xingu Indian Park. This reserve has provided many Indian tribes with a place to take refuge from the invaders of their lands. It also protects them from non-Indian settlers.

Things to do

Decorative designs

Here are some of the many different designs that Amazon Indians weave into their baskets or paint onto other objects. On page 29 there is a photograph of a newly woven loincloth being decorated with black paint for a Panare initiation ceremony. Amazon Indians normally use the black or red paint that is obtainable from forest plants.

You could decorate cards, posters, clothing material, and many other things, with the above designs. The easiest way to use a design more than once is by making potato stamps. You will need: a large potato; a sharp knife; a dark felt-tip pen; a paint brush; water-colour paint or dye, and some paper or other material. Now follow the instructions.

1 Cut a large potato in half, making sure that the surface is flat.

2 Draw the outline of a design onto the flat surface of the potato.

3 Carefully cut out the area around the design with a knife.

4 Brush the colour you choose onto the outstanding surface.

5 Press the painted surface onto the paper, applying more paint when needed.

Paper mâché masks

On page 33 there is a photograph of two Indians wearing straw costumes and face masks. By following the instructions in this section, you could make a similar face mask of your own. You will need: newspaper; some bowls; plasticine; liquid glue or cellulose wallpaper paste; a board; vaseline; tempera paint; and a piece of elastic cord about 4 cm long.

1 Leave some pieces of newspaper to soak in a bowl of water for about four hours.

2 In the meantime, shape the face you want to give the mask in plasticine.

3 Take the pieces of newspaper out of the water and squeeze them in your hands to remove the liquid.

4 Mix the newspaper pulp with the glue or paste. Then place the sticky mixture on a board.

5 Cover your plasticine model with a thin layer of vaseline grease to prevent the paper from sticking to it.

6 Cover the model with about 3 mm of paper. Allow the paper to dry for 6-8 hours and then remove it in one piece.

7 Mix a small amount of glue with tempera paint. Then decorate the mask with the paint in whatever way you like.

8 Knot the elastic cord through a hole on both sides of the mask so that you can wear it on your head.

The Panare hoop game

Panare boys play a hoop game called 'patai'. They make a hoop out of a liana (a woody, climbing plant). Then one boy puts a long stick through the hoop and whirls it around in the air. He hurls it at another boy, making it bounce on the way. The other boy catches the hoop with his stick and hurls it back.

You can also play this game by using an old bicycle tyre as a hoop. Ask a friend to stand about 25 metres away. Whirl the tyre around at about shoulder height. When it has got up speed, hurl it towards your friend, making it bounce on the ground on the way. (It will take some practice to become good at this.) Your friend must send it back to you.

Reference

South American Indian languages

It is estimated that more than 300 languages are spoken by the Indians of South America. Most of these languages are spoken by the Indian tribes that live in and around the Amazon Basin.

Language families and groups
If several languages are fairly similar to one another, they are said to belong to the same 'language group'. For example, English, Dutch, German and several Scandinavian languages are said to belong to the Germanic language group; French, Spanish and Italian belong to the Romance language group. When languages belonging to different language groups share some similarities—for example, English is similar to French but totally different from Chinese—the groups are said to belong to the same 'language family'.

The Indian languages of the Amazon Basin belong to three large language families. The many different languages in all the language groups in each family have developed over thousands of years from one parent language. So, the Indian tribes that speak the languages belonging to one language group usually live in the same geographical area. The four largest language groups, and their main areas, are listed below. Look them up on the maps on pages 4 and 13.

1 Tupi—along the Atlantic coast of Brazil and the lower stretch of the Amazon River towards the mouth.
2 Carib—in the Guiana Highlands.
3 Arawak—in the north-west Amazon and along the eastern foothills of the Andes.
4 Ge—in the grassland areas of central Brazil.

However, in each of these four main areas, languages belonging to other language groups are also spoken, as well as European languages spoken by non-Indians. Today, in all parts of the Amazon Basin, except for the most isolated, there are many more speakers of European languages than of Indian languages. Very few Amazon Indian languages are spoken by more than 10,000 people. Some are spoken by less than 20 people and these are likely to die out soon as the tribes adopt the customs of the non-Indians.

Comparisons
Many people who live in modern industrial societies believe that, because the way of life of tribal peoples is simpler than their own, their languages must be simpler too. This is not strictly true. English, for example, is said to have the largest vocabulary in the world. This is mainly because English is spoken all over the world by peoples whose ways of life are very different—they therefore need to use different terms. In contrast, an Amazon Indian language is spoken by a much smaller number of people living in the same general area. So they only need to use one set of terms.

Also, Amazon Indians do not need to use the large number of technical and scientific terms that exist in modern industrial societies. But all Indians know the names of hundreds of different types of trees, animals, fish and birds, on which they depend for food or for the materials to make weapons and many other things. The vocabulary of most English-speaking people (excluding scientific specialists) is not as large as it could be—it is probably no larger than the vocabulary of an Amazon Indian.

The grammar of some Amazon Indian languages can be more complicated than English grammar. In the Panare language (belonging to the Carib group), there are many more past tenses than there are in English. The tense used to describe some past event depends on how long ago that event took place. For example, different tenses would be used to describe an event that happened a week ago and one that happened a year ago.

Glossary

Curare The poison which Amazon Indians make from a wild forest plant and apply to the darts they use in blowpipes.

Gourd A large, hard-rinded, fleshy fruit.

Initiation The ceremony of entering a group or society. The initiation of an Amazon Indian girl or boy is when he or she is ready to enter adulthood.

Liana A woody, climbing plant, particularly found in tropical forests.

Manioc A plant which has a root that forms the most important part of the Indians' diet. It can be boiled or turned into flour from which bread is made.

Papaya A tree that bears a fruit (also called papaya) which the Amazon Indians eat. Also referred to as 'paw-paw'.

Percussion instrument An instrument which has to be struck by the player, like a drum.

Shaman Among Amazon Indian tribes, a person who is believed to know a lot about the spirits and can therefore cure people who have been made ill by them. Also referred to as a 'witch doctor' or 'medicine man'.

Tribe A group of people who share the same language and culture. The members of an Amazon Indian tribe nearly always divide up into more than one village in the same region.

Tributary A stream or river that runs into another.

Universe The whole world, including the sky.

Yam A plant which has a root that is an important part of the Amazon Indians' diet.

Important dates

about 15,000 BC First Indians arrived in South America.

about 5,000 BC Manioc first cultivated in South America.

AD 1492 Christopher Columbus and his men arrived in the Bahamas; the first Europeans to meet South American Indians.

1500 Pero Alvares Cabral arrived off the coast of Brazil.

1542 New Laws passed, forbidding the enslavement of Indians in Spanish colonies. But Spanish authorities unable to enforce them. Also first ascent of Amazon by Spaniards.

1759 Jesuit missionaries expelled from Portuguese colonies. Eight years later, also expelled from Spanish colonies. The kings of Spain and Portugal felt the Jesuits were getting too powerful through control over Indians.

1821 After the war by which the Spanish colonies gained independence from Spain, Indians declared full citizens of the new republics. But the Amazon Indians' relations with non-Indians did not improve.

1910 Indian Protection Service established in Brazil. Recognized that Indians had a right to live according to their own traditions, but expected them to change with time. In most other countries, Indian affairs mostly controlled by missionaries.

1959 Xingu Indian Park established and administered by Claudio and Orlando Villas Boas. These brothers dedicated most of their lives to helping the Indians.

1967 Indian Protection Service stopped because its employees had been bribed into allowing Indian lands to be stolen and Indian villages to be attacked. Replaced by the present Brazilian government organization responsible for Indian affairs, the National Indian Foundation (FUNAI).

1973 Statute of the Indian passed into Brazilian Law. In theory, but not in practice, it safeguards the Indians' rights over their traditional homelands.

Books

A Closer Look at Amazonian Indians by Stephen Hugh Jones (Hamish Hamilton). A description of the life of the Barasana Indians of southern Colombia.

For older readers and adults:
The Gentle People by Colin Henfrey (Hutchinson); *Wai-wai* by Nicholas Guppy (John Murray). Both these books are accounts of visits made to Indian tribes of Guyana.
The Cocaine Eaters by Brian Moser and Donald Tayler (Longman). An account of visits to several tribes of Colombia.
The Savage and the Innocent by David Maybury-Lewis (Evans). An account of the experiences of an anthropologist who, accompanied by his wife and small son, went to study the Shavante of central Brazil.
Xingu : the Indians, their myths by Claudio and Orlando Villas Boas; translated by Kenneth Brecher (Souvenir Press). A collection of myths as told by the Indians of the Xingu Indian Park to the Villas Boas brothers.
Red Gold : the conquest of the Brazilian Indians by John Hemming (Macmillan). An explanation of how the Portuguese occupied half of South America, and how countless Indian tribes died as a result.
Native Peoples of South America by Julian Steward and Louis Faron (McGraw-Hill). The only summary of all that was known about South American Indians in the late 1950s.
A Question of Survival by Robin Hanbury-Tenison (Angus and Robertson). An account of the visit made by the author to the Indians of Brazil, at the request of the Brazilian government, to examine the problems caused by the Indians' contact with the modern world.
The Heart of the Forest by Adrian Cowell (Gollancz). The author's description of his journey with Orlando Villas Boas to the unexplored Xingu region.

Some of the above books are out of print but they should still be available from the main public libraries.

Films for hire

The Last of the Cuiva (Granada TV). The conflict between cattle ranchers and a group of Indians living on the Venezuelan-Colombian border.
War of the Gods (Granada TV). The effects of missionaries on the Barasana and Maku Indians.
The Sound of Rushing Water. A film made by the Shuar Indians with the technical help of non-Indians. It tells the history of the Shuar's resistance to conquest by outsiders and describes their present efforts to defend their land rights in the face of invasion by non-Indians.
The Tribe that Hides from Man (Adrian Cowell); *The Kingdom in the Jungle* (Adrian Cowell); *Contact with a Hostile Tribe* (BBC TV). These three films deal with the work of the Villas Boas brothers in the Xingu Indian Park of central Brazil.

All these films can be hired from Survival International.

Survival International

A London-based charity that publicizes the present predicament of tribal peoples all over the world and finds funds for small-scale projects to help them. Survival International has a special interest in South American Indians. Further information about its work can be obtained from its head office at: 36 Craven Street, London WC2N 5NG. Tel. no: 01-839 3267.

Index